Small Business Administration Trade and Export Promotion Programs

Sean Lowry
Analyst in Public Finance

January 22, 2014

Congressional Research Service

7-5700
www.crs.gov
R43155

Summary

According to Census data, approximately 1% of small businesses in the United States currently export. With roughly three-quarters of world purchasing power and almost 95% of world consumers living outside of U.S. borders, more attention is being paid to the potential of small business export promotion programs to grow small businesses and contribute to the national economic recovery. In addition, some Members of Congress believe that the contributions of small businesses to commercial innovation and economic growth could be enhanced through greater access to growing international markets.

Consistent with these policy goals, the Small Business Administration (SBA) provides export promotion and financing services to small businesses through its loan guarantee programs, management and training programs, and other initiatives. SBA's Office of International Trade (OIT) coordinates these activities as it assists with four stages of export promotion: (1) identifying small businesses interested in export promotion; (2) preparing small businesses to export; (3) connecting small businesses to export opportunities; and (4) supporting small businesses once they find export opportunities.

The Small Business Jobs Act of 2010 (P.L. 111-240) elevated trade within SBA by establishing an Assistant Administrator to lead OIT and report directly to the SBA Administrator. The act also authorized SBA to establish a three-year State Trade and Export Promotion (STEP) Pilot Grant Initiative. Under the STEP initiative, which was appropriated $30 million both in FY2011 and FY2012, SBA awarded grants to states with the goal of assisting eligible "small business concerns" with exporting. The STEP program's authorization expired at the end of FY2013. On January 17, 2014, the President signed into law the Consolidated Appropriations Act, 2014 (H.R. 3547), which appropriated $8 million for the STEP program in FY2014.

SBA's export-related loans amounted to approximately $1.2 billion (comprising approximately 5.0% of SBA's annual loan portfolio) in FY2013. Although SBA has three loan programs that are specifically targeted toward exporters, many of SBA's broader loan programs support export-related activities. Surveys indicate that relatively few clients of SBA's management and training programs request trade-related counseling, and some choose to receive this information from other federal programs (such as those provided by the Department of Commerce).

This report begins with the history, role, and scope of SBA's export promotion activities, and the creation of OIT. Next, quantitative data from SBA and qualitative data from other sources are used to provide performance analysis of SBA's international programs.

This report concludes with a presentation of three issues for consideration during an era where concerns of fiscal responsibility and economic recovery are high priorities for many policy makers. First, are there market barriers impeding smaller firms from exporting? Second, is there a compelling interest for the government to promote exports in the name of national "competitiveness"? Third, are SBA's export-promotion policies duplicative of other federal programs? In the 113th Congress, several bills have been introduced to improve efficiencies among small business export promotion programs (e.g., H.R. 1909, H.R. 1926, H.R. 1916, S. 1179).

Contents

Introduction 1
SBA's Office of International Trade 2
Export Promotion-Focused Loan Programs 5
Export-Related Aspects of Management and Training Programs 8
State Trade and Export Promotion (STEP) Grants 8
Data Analysis of Performance 10
    Loan Programs 10
    Survey Responses 14
Issues for Congress 17
    Small Business Barriers to Exporting and Possible Market Failures 17
    Small Business Exports and U.S. Trade "Competitiveness" 18
    Duplication of Services 20

Tables

Table 1. SBA's Office of International Trade Total Program Costs, FY2007-FY2014 4
Table 2. Key Features of SBA's Three Export Promotion Loan Programs 6
Table 3. SBA Approved Loans for Export-Related Activity, FY2011 to FY2013 11
Table 4. SBA Loan Program Approvals for Export-Related Activity, by Loan Program, FY2011- FY2013 12
Table 5. SBA Loan Program Approval Amounts for Export-Related Activity, by Loan Program, FY2011- FY2013 13
Table 6. Exporter Survey Responses on SBA International Trade Programs 16

Appendixes

Appendix. A Brief Description of SBA Loan Programs Used to Support Export Activities 23

Contacts

Author Contact Information 23

Introduction

Some Members of Congress believe that the contributions of small businesses to commercial innovation and economic growth could be enhanced through greater access to growing international markets. In 2010, the U.S. International Trade Commission (USITC) reported that about 97% of businesses (i.e., firms with fewer than 500 workers) are small, but these small businesses accounted for only about 30% of known U.S. merchandise exports between 1997 and 2007.[1] During this period, the value of small businesses' merchandise exports increased from $152.9 billion to $306.6 billion (100.5%), compared with an increase of $385.1 billion to $719.2 billion (86.7%) among larger firms. However, the benefits of exporting are shared among a small segment of small businesses.

According to Census data, approximately 1% of small businesses in the United States export.[2] With roughly three-quarters of world purchasing power and almost 95% of world consumers living outside of U.S. borders, more attention is being paid to the potential of small business export promotion programs to contribute to the national economic recovery.[3]

Expanding small business exports is also part of President Obama's economic policy agenda. In 2010, President Obama launched the National Export Initiative (NEI), a strategy for doubling U.S. exports by the end of 2014 to support U.S. job creation. The President's FY2014 budget request emphasized the role of small business in fulfilling the NEI:

> A critical component of stimulating domestic economic growth is ensuring that U.S. businesses can actively participate in international markets and increase their exports of goods and services ... The NEI advances the Administration's goal of doubling exports over five years by ... helping firms—especially small businesses—overcome the hurdles to entering new export markets, assisting with trade financing, and pursuing a Government-wide approach to export advocacy abroad.[4]

Economists generally do not view job creation as a justification for providing federal assistance to small businesses.[5] They argue that in the long term such assistance will likely reallocate jobs

---

[1] See Letter from Ron Kirk, U.S. Trade Representative, to The Honorable Shara L. Aranoff, Chair of the U.S. International Trade Commission, October 5, 2009, in U.S. International Trade Commission, *Small and Medium-Sized Enterprises: Overview of Participation in U.S. Exports*, January 2010, at http://www.usitc.gov/publications/332/pub4125.pdf. USITC refers to businesses with fewer than 500 workers as a "small or medium sized enterprise" (SME). USITC's size standard for an "SME" is similar to the Small Business Administration's most common size standard for determining whether a firm is a "small business." See CRS Report R40860, *Small Business Size Standards: A Historical Analysis of Contemporary Issues*, by Robert Jay Dilger.

[2] According to CRS analysis of Census data from 2008, approximately 1.53% of employer firms with fewer than 500 employees exported. If non-employer firms are incorporated into this calculation, then 0.72% of firms with fewer than 500 employees exported in 2008. See U.S. Census Bureau, 2008 Profile of U.S. Exporting Companies, Exhibit 1a, April 13, 2010, at http://www.census.gov/foreign-trade/Press-Release/edb/2008/; and Statistics about Business Size (2008), Table 2a, at http://www.census.gov/econ/smallbus.html.

[3] Office of the United States Trade Representative, *Economy and Trade*, at http://www.ustr.gov/trade-topics/economy-trade.

[4] Office of Management and Budget, *Fiscal Year 2014 Budget of the U.S. Government*, April 2013, p. 135, at http://www.whitehouse.gov/sites/default/files/omb/budget/fy2014/assets/budget.pdf.

[5] For further information reviewing the theoretical arguments and empirical literature on small business and job creation, see CRS Report R41392, *Small Business and the Expiration of the 2001 Tax Rate Reductions: Economic Issues*, by Jane G. Gravelle and Sean Lowry; CRS Report RL32254, *Small Business Tax Benefits: Current Law and* (continued...)

within the economy, not increase them. In their view, jobs arise primarily from the size of the labor force, which depends largely on population, demographics, and factors that affect the choice of home versus market production (e.g., the entry of women in the workforce). However, economic theory does suggest that increased federal spending on small business assistance programs may result in additional jobs in the short term.

Why do some emphasize export promotion assistance to small business? Advocates for more federal small business export promotion assistance argue that helping small businesses to export will lead to more jobs. A commonly held view is that small businesses are the major source of job creation in the U.S. economy, and thus policy makers should try to encourage the growth of small businesses as a means to increase employment. Economists have debated for decades the extent to which small businesses contribute to job creation.[6] Recent empirical studies indicate that small business owners have different aspirations concerning the growth of their firm, and small, new firms (i.e., startups) are more likely to expand than small businesses, generally.

This report begins with the history, role, and scope of the Small Business Administration's (SBA's) export promotion activities, and the creation of SBA's Office of International Trade (OIT). OIT is charged with coordinating SBA's export promotion activities, including management and training programs, grants, and loan programs. Next, the report describes the three major forms of SBA trade-related assistance: (1) export promotion-focused loans, (2) management and training programs, and (3) the State Trade and Export Promotion Pilot Grant Initiative to the states (which expired in 2013). This report then uses quantitative data from SBA and qualitative data from surveys and federal auditors (i.e., the Government Accountability Office and the SBA Office of Inspector General) to present performance analysis of SBA's international programs.

Three policy issues for Congress are also discussed. First, are there market barriers impeding smaller firms from exporting? Second, is there a compelling interest for the government to promote exports in the name of national "competitiveness"? Third, are SBA's export-promotion policies duplicative of other federal programs? These policy issues could arise in future debates over the size and scope of SBA's international trade programs. This debate will likely be framed by the issues of fiscal responsibility and economic recovery.

SBA's Office of International Trade

SBA provides export promotion and financing services to small businesses through its business loan programs, management and training programs, and other initiatives. SBA's OIT coordinates these activities as it assists with four stages of export promotion: (1) identifying small businesses interested in export promotion, (2) preparing small businesses to export, (3) connecting small businesses to export opportunities, and (4) supporting small businesses once they find export

---

(...continued)
Main Arguments For and Against Them, by Gary Guenther; and CRS Report R41523, *Small Business Administration and Job Creation*, by Robert Jay Dilger.

[6] For more discussion of the debate among researchers on small business and job creation, see CRS Report R41523, *Small Business Administration and Job Creation*, by Robert Jay Dilger and CRS Report R41392, *Small Business and the Expiration of the 2001 Tax Rate Reductions: Economic Issues*, by Jane G. Gravelle and Sean Lowry.

opportunities. SBA also participates in the regional network of U.S. Export Assistance Centers, which are managed by the Department of Commerce's International Trade Administration.[7]

Despite its name, OIT primarily encourages export promotion rather than international trade, generally. None of OIT's programs have a specific goal to help small businesses gain access to lower-cost or specialized imports, such as for use as inputs in their production processes.[8] This export-oriented focus is consistent with other federal agencies.[9]

OIT's programs are funded through a combination of the SBA's appropriations for business loan programs (i.e., subsidy costs) and for salaries and expenses. Congress does not directly provide an appropriation amount for each of the SBA's three export-focused loan programs or trade-related counseling provided through SBA's management and training programs.

Table 1 provides OIT's total program costs from FY2007 to FY2013 and the President's budget request for FY2014. Total program costs include obligations covering the full cost for administering OIT's major programs and services. This includes direct costs from the operating budget plus compensation and benefits; agency-wide costs, such as rent and telecommunications; and indirect costs, such as agency overhead (e.g., financial management). In terms of scale, OIT's total program costs of $8.9 million in FY2012 accounted for approximately 1.5% of SBA's total program obligations for the year (not including disaster assistance).[10] For FY2013, OIT's total program costs were approximately $9.8 million.[11] For FY2014, the President requested that funding for OIT's programs increase by approximately 30.9%, to $12.8 million.

---

[7] For more information on the Department of Commerce's export promotion programs, see CRS Report R41495, *U.S. Government Agencies Involved in Export Promotion: Overview and Issues for Congress*, coordinated by Shayerah Ilias Akhtar.

[8] It appears, however, that some SBA management and training programs are capable of providing this sort of counseling to their small business clients. For example, see Caron Beesley, "Importing Goods into the U.S.—An Introductory Guide for Small Business Owners," U.S. Small Business Administration, July 3, 2012, at http://www.sba.gov/community/blogs/importing-goods-us-%E2%80%93-introductory-guide-small-business-owners.

[9] The economic theory supporting the justifications for export promotion programs is discussed in more depth in the "Issues for Congress" section of this report. The implicit rationale for the emphasis on export promotion is that exports support job creation in the United States. However, comparative advantage theory in economics indicates exports from foreign countries help those countries pay for imports from the United States and that voluntary trade occurs because it is mutually beneficial to all parties involved. See Federal Reserve Bank of Dallas, *The Fruits of Free Trade*, 2002, at https://www.dallasfed.org/assets/documents/fed/annual/2002/ar02.pdf. In addition, given the nature of global supply chains, foreign imports into the United States could also contain some intermediate components made in the United States. For example, see Galina Hale and Bart Hobijn, "The U.S. Content of 'Made in China,'" *Federal Reserve Bank of San Francisco, Economic Letter*, August 8, 2011, at http://www.frbsf.org/economic-research/files/el2011-25.pdf.

[10] According to SBA, its total program obligations were approximately $802.5 million in FY2012 ($215.6 million of which was for disaster assistance). See U.S. Small Business Administration, *FY2014 Congressional Budget Justification and FY2012 Annual Performance Report*, p. 29, at http://www.sba.gov/sites/default/files/files/1-508-Compliant-FY-2014-CBJ%20FY%202012%20APR.pdf. See also footnote 8 for more information on how these program costs are organized in SBA's annual budget justification.

[11] This amount does not include the majority of program costs associated with making export-related loans, which are largely included under the total program costs for "capital access programs" in SBA's annual budget justification. See the notes in **Table 1** for more information.

Table 1. SBA's Office of International Trade Total Program Costs, FY2007-FY2014

Fiscal Year	Total Program Costs[a] (in thousands of dollars)
FY2014 (request)	$12,807
FY2013	$9,787[b]
FY2012	$8,943
FY2011	$7,681
FY2010	$8,016
FY2009	$4,660
FY2008	$4,154
FY2007	$5,258

Sources: U.S. Small Business Administration, *FY2014 Congressional Budget Justification and FY2012 Annual Performance Report*, pp. 28 and 62, at http://www.sba.gov/sites/default/files/files/1-508-Compliant-FY-2014-CBJ%20FY%202012%20APR.pdf.

a. These amounts include direct costs from the operating budget plus compensation and benefits; agency-wide costs, such as rent and telecommunications; and indirect costs, such as agency overhead (e.g., financial management). In a telephone call with CRS on June 12, 2013, SBA indicated that approximately 90% of the cost of issuing export-related loans is captured under the total program costs for "Capital Access Programs."

b. Across-the-board spending cuts in FY2013 (e.g., sequestration) apply at the level of "programs, projects, and activities" (PPA). Because OIT's funding is organized below the level of PPA, SBA is not required to apply these spending reductions across the board to OIT's budget. SBA confirmed to CRS that it did not plan to reduce OIT's budget as part of its efforts to comply with agency spending caps in FY2013.

Before December 2010, OIT was a division within SBA's Office of Capital Access. It was led by the Director for International Trade, who reported to the Associate Administrator (AA) for Capital Access. The Small Business Jobs Act of 2010 (P.L. 111-240) required the SBA Administrator to appoint an AA for International Trade no later than December 27, 2010. Accordingly, OIT's reporting structure was realigned such that the AA for International Trade now reports directly to the Office of the SBA Administrator. On December 23, 2010, the SBA Administrator approved the reorganization that included the formation of the OIT and appointed the first AA for International Trade in August 2011. These administrative changes were intended to raise the profile of SBA's export promotion activities within the agency.

SBA is one of several federal agencies that assist in the promotion of small business exports, and export promotion more generally.[12] SBA's website provides a table of federal programs that help to finance small business exports.[13] Most of these federal programs are located within other organizations, such as the Export-Import Bank of the United States, the Department of Commerce, the Department of Agriculture, the U.S. Trade and Development Agency, and the Overseas Private Investment Corporation.

---

[12] For a summary of these other federal export promotion activities, see CRS Report R41495, *U.S. Government Agencies Involved in Export Promotion: Overview and Issues for Congress*, coordinated by Shayerah Ilias Akhtar.

[13] U.S. Small Business Administration, "Financing your Small Business Exports, Foreign Investments or Projects," at http://www.sba.gov/content/financing-your-small-business-exports-foreign-investments-or-projects.

SBA is also member of the Trade Promotion Coordinating Committee (TPCC), an interagency committee whose objective is to coordinate and set priorities for federal agencies involved in export promotion. The TPCC then proposes a unified export promotion budget to the President. The TPCC is composed of 20-member agencies, including the Department of Commerce, the Export-Import Bank, SBA, the Department of State, the U.S. Trade Representative, and the Department of the Treasury. The Secretary of Commerce chairs the TPCC.[14]

Export Promotion-Focused Loan Programs

SBA identifies small businesses interested in export promotion through a combination of informational and financial programs. Technically speaking, any of SBA's loan programs can be used for firms looking to begin exporting or expand their current exporting operations. Indeed, many of SBA's loan programs contribute to this mission (analyzed in the "Data Analysis of Performance" section).

SBA has three loan programs that specifically focus on export promotion:

- *Export Express loan program*, which provides working capital or fixed asset financing for firms that will begin or expand exporting;

- *Export Working Capital loan program*, which provides financing to support export orders or the export transaction cycle, from purchase order to final payment; and

- *International Trade loan program*, which provides long-term financing to support firms that are expanding because of growing export sales or have been adversely affected by imports and need to modernize to meet foreign competition.

Table 2 summarizes the key features of SBA's three export promotion-focused loan programs.

---

[14] For more information, see CRS Report R41495, *U.S. Government Agencies Involved in Export Promotion: Overview and Issues for Congress*, coordinated by Shayerah Ilias Akhtar.

Table 2. Key Features of SBA's Three Export Promotion Loan Programs

Key Feature	Export Express Loan Program	Export Working Capital Program	International Trade Loan Program
Who qualifies?	Small business applicant must demonstrate that the loan will enable them to enter a new, or expand in, an existing export market. Business must have been in operation for at least 12 months (though not necessarily in exporting).	[Same as 7(a) loan program] Must be an eligible, for-profit business; meet SBA size standards; and show "good character," credit, management, and ability to repay	[Same as 7(a) loan program] Applicants must be an eligible, for-profit business; meet SBA size standards; and show "good character," credit, management, and ability to repay. Also, applicants must be engaged or preparing to engage in international trade/adversely affected by competition from imports.
Use of proceeds	[Same as SBAExpress loan program] Revolving lines of credit (up to seven years in maturity) or for a term loan for export transactions, including support for standby letters of credit; export development expenses, including trade show participation; and translation of product literature	Short-term, working-capital loans to support export orders or the export transaction cycle, from purchase order to final payment. May be transaction based or asset based. Eligible proceeds include raw materials, inventory, labor, and the resulting foreign accounts receivable; overhead costs incurred to fulfill an export sales order; or standby letters of credit.	Term loans for permanent working capital (e.g., raw materials), equipment, facilities, land and buildings, and debt refinance related to international trade
Maximum loan amount	Gross loan amount limited to $500,000 per loan. SBA guaranty amount limited to $450,000 to one borrower (and any affiliates)	Gross loan amount limited to $5 million per loan. SBA guaranty amount limited to $4.5 million to one borrower (and any affiliates)	The gross loan amount is limited to $5 million per loan. SBA guaranty amount limited to $4.5 million to one borrower (and any affiliates). However, the amount guaranteed for working capital for the International Trade loan combined with any other outstanding 7(a) loan for working capital cannot exceed $4 million.
Maturity	[Same as SBAExpress loan program] Terms up to 25 years for fixed assets and up to seven years for revolving lines of credit for working capital	Generally one year or less, but may go up to three years	Up to 25 years
Graduated Fee Rate Structure	(Fee charged on guarantied portion of loan only)		
	[Same as 7(a) loan program] Maturity one year or less: 0.25% guaranty fee; Maturity over one year: $150,000 or less = For FY2014, the SBA is not charging an upfront guaranty or an annual servicing fee; $150,001-$700,000 gross amount = 3.0%; $700,001-$1 million = 3.5%; and 3.75% on any portion over $1 million. Ongoing fee of 0.52%	[Same as 7(a) loan program]	[Same as 7(a) loan program]

Key Feature	Export Express Loan Program	Export Working Capital Program	International Trade Loan Program
Maximum interest rates	[Same as SBAExpress loan program] Loans $50,000 or less: prime + 6.5%; Loans over $50,000: prime + 4.5%	No SBA maximum interest rate cap, but SBA monitors for "reasonableness"	[Same as 7(a) loan program] Loans less than seven years: $0-$25,000 = prime +4.25%; $25,001-$50,000 = prime + 3.25%; over $50,000 = prime + 2.25% Loans seven years or longer: $0-$25,000 = prime +4.75%; $25,001-$50,000 = prime + 3.75%; over $50,000 = prime + 2.75%
Percentage of guaranty	90% guaranty for loans of $350,000 or less; 75% guaranty for loans greater than $350,000	90% guaranty not to exceed $4.5 million	90% guaranty not to exceed $4.5 million (up to $4 million maximum guaranty for working capital)

Source: U.S. Small Business Administration, *Loan Program Quick Reference Guide*, June 2012, at http://www.sba.gov/content/loan-program-quick-reference-guide.

For FY2014, the SBA is not charging an upfront guaranty fee or an annual servicing fee for 7(a) or export loans in the amount of $150,000 or less. Because the fees are zero, lenders may not charge a guaranty fee to the borrower.[15]

In addition to these export promotion-focused programs, SBA also supports small business exports through its other business loan programs. These programs include the 504/CDC program, standard 7(a) program, and specialized 7(a) programs (see the **Appendix** for a brief summary of these loan programs). The size of the export activity within each of these programs is discussed in the "Data Analysis of Performance" section of this report.

In many ways, SBA's export promotion loan programs share similar characteristics to other SBA loan programs. For example, the Export Express program resembles the SBA*Express* program. The SBA*Express* shares several of the characteristics of the standard 7(a) loan guarantee program except that it has an expedited approval process (which increases the risk of loan losses), a lower maximum loan amount, and a smaller percentage of the loan guaranteed (which both reduce SBA's exposure to potential losses).[16] Similarly, the Export Express program shares several of the characteristics of the standard International Trade loan program, such as an expedited approval

---

[15] U.S. Small Business Administration, "SBA Information Notice: 7(a) and 504 Fees Effective On October 1, 2013," at http://www.sba.gov/sites/default/files/5000-1288.pdf. An email from SBA to CRS, dated 10/30/13, confirmed that the exemption applied to international trade loans of $150,000 of less.

[16] SBAExpress has an expedited loan approval process which some have argued increases the risk of loan losses. For example, the SBA's Office of Inspector General has reported that just over half of the loan dollars guaranteed by the SBA in FY2011 were made using delegated authorities and that although the SBA has made some progress in improving its oversight procedures of these lenders, the agency does not always recognize the significance of lender weaknesses and the corresponding risk they pose for loan losses. See U.S. Small Business Administration Office of Inspector General, *Report on the Most Serious Management and Performance Challenges*, Report No. 13-02, October 15, 2012, p. 5, at http://www.sba.gov/sites/default/files/FY%202013%20Management%20Challenges%20OIG%20Report%2013-02%20.pdf. The percentage of guarantee is 50% under SBA*Express* program instead of a maximum of 75% or 85% under the standard 7(a) program.

process in exchange for a lower maximum loan amount ($500,000 compared with $5 million) and a lower percentage of guaranty.[17]

Export-Related Aspects of Management and Training Programs

SBA provides trade-related counseling to small business owners through its management and training programs as well as through its participation in inter-agency counseling programs. Small Business Development Centers (SBDCs) are the largest SBA source of trade-related counseling. SBA also offers counseling through other programs, such as Women's Business Centers (WBCs) and the Service Corps of Retired Executives (SCORE).[18]

SBA also partners with other agencies to provide small business export counseling. For example, SBA provides small business counselor training certification program and engages in counseling services to small business in partnership with the Department of Commerce-led U.S. Export Assistance Centers (USEACs). As of the end of FY2012, SBA had counseled 4,595 small business owners and trained 10,598 small business owners on export finance at various USEACs.[19]

State Trade and Export Promotion (STEP) Grants

The Small Business Jobs Act of 2010 authorized SBA to establish a three-year State Trade and Export Promotion (STEP) Pilot Grant Initiative. Congress appropriated funding for the program for two years: $30 million in FY2011 and $30 million in FY2012. On January 17, 2014, the President signed into law the Consolidated Appropriations Act, 2014 (H.R. 3547), which appropriated $8 million for the STEP program in FY2014.

Under the STEP initiative, the SBA awarded grants to states in FY2011 and FY2012 with the goal of assisting eligible "small business concerns" with exporting.[20] The program's objectives were to

---

[17] The percentage of guarantee is 75%/90% under the Export Express program versus 90% for the International Trade and Export Working Capital loan programs. The 90% guaranty for SBA's Export Working Capital loan program is similar to the 90% guaranty in the Export-Import Bank's (Ex-Im) Working Capital Guarantee program. However, Ex-Im's program differs slightly from SBA's (e.g., no limit on loans compared to SBA's limit of $5 million). For more information comparing these programs, see U.S. Government Accountability Office, *2013 Annual Report: Actions Needed to Reduce Fragmentation, Overlap, Duplication, and Achieve Other Financial Benefits*, GAO-13-279SP, April 2013, p. 112, at http://www.gao.gov/assets/660/653604.pdf.

[18] SBDCs provide a vast array of technical assistance to small businesses and aspiring entrepreneurs. WBCs represent a national network of educational centers designed to assist women start and grow small businesses. SCORE is a nonprofit association dedicated to entrepreneur education where working and retired executives and business owners donate their time and expertise as volunteer business counselors and provide confidential counseling and mentoring free of charge. For more information on these programs, see CRS Report R41352, *Small Business Management and Technical Assistance Training Programs*, by Robert Jay Dilger.

[19] U.S. Small Business Administration, *FY2014 Congressional Budget Justification and FY2012 Annual Performance Report*, p. 63, at http://www.sba.gov/sites/default/files/files/1-508-Compliant-FY-2014-CBJ%20FY%202012%20APR.pdf.

[20] Small business concerns that are eligible to participate in STEP activities must be in business for more than one year; operate profitably; demonstrate an understanding of costs associated with exporting; possess a strategic plan for (continued...)

(1) increase the number of eligible small business concerns in the state that export and (2) increase the export volume of those eligible small businesses that already export. SBA awarded STEP grants to states to execute export programs that assist eligible small business concerns in

- participation in a foreign trade mission;
- a foreign market sales trip;
- a subscription to services provided by the U.S. Department of Commerce;
- the payment of website translation fees;
- the design of international marketing media;
- a trade show exhibition;
- participation in training workshops; or
- any other export initiative determined appropriate by the AA for SBA Office of International Trade.

Under the first grant competition in 2011, SBA awarded 51 cooperative agreements, totaling $28,977,094. Under the second competition in 2012, the agency awarded 52 cooperative agreements, totaling $29,996,182. Individual state project award amounts varied based on proposed project plans and budgets. In the first grant competition, the average award was $568,000. In the second grant competition, the average award was $577,000.[21] Some of the projects that SBA prioritized in awarding the grants included assistance to eligible small business concerns that are owned and controlled by socially and economically disadvantaged individuals; women-owned; veteran- or service- disabled veteran-owned; located in rural areas; new-to market export opportunities to the People's Republic of China; or part of a regional, industry-focused, innovation clusters.[22]

SBA was authorized to competitively award STEP grants to the 50 states, District of Columbia, Commonwealth of Puerto Rico, Virgin Islands, Guam, American Samoa, and the Northern Mariana Islands.[23] Under the STEP initiative, in most cases SBA provided 75% of the funding required for the total project, and states provided 25%. However, for the top three states in value of exports, SBA provided 65% of total funding, whereas these states provided 35%.[24]

The STEP program was the subject of an audit by the SBA Office of Inspector General (OIG) of the overall management and effectiveness of the program during the first year of the program

---

(...continued)

exporting; and meet small business size requirements as defined in 13 CFR 121.

[21] U.S. Small Business Administration, State Trade and Export Promotion (STEP) Pilot Grant Initiative, CFDA# 59.061, at http://www.sba.gov/content/state-trade-and-export-promotion-step-grants-pilot.

[22] For information about the initial round (FY2011-FY2013) of STEP award amounts by state and a summary of each state's activity, see U.S. Small Business Administration, "State Trade and Export Promotion (STEP) Program Fact Sheet," at http://www.sba.gov/content/state-trade-and-export-promotion-step-fact-sheet.

[23] Section 1699(a) of the National Defense Authorization Act for Fiscal Year 2013 (P.L. 112-239) added the Northern Mariana Islands to the definition of eligible "states" for STEP.

[24] U.S. Small Business Administration, Fact Sheet – U.S. Small Business Administration Office of International Trade State Trade and Export Promotion Grant Program, Program Announcement No. OIT-STEP-2012-01, at http://www.sba.gov/sites/default/files/files/STEP%202012%20PROGRAM%20ANNOUNCEMENT%20FACT%20SHEET%20MARCH%2027%202012.pdf.

(FY2011).[25] According to the Small Business Jobs Act of 2010, SBA was required to report to Congress "the effect of each grant on exports" in the state receiving the grant. OIG emphasized that there was a the lack of established baselines to measure changes in a state's small business exporters or exports among some initial grant recipients, and OIG argued that the program's performance goals were not specific and results-oriented.[26] OIG also found that some states focused on goals that did not directly increase the number of small business exporters or the export volume of existing small business exporters. Following SBA's agency comments on the study, OIG determined that SBA management was responsive to several issues raised in the report as SBA prepared its FY2012 round of STEP awards.

Data Analysis of Performance

This section analyzes export-related performance data for SBA's business loan and management and training programs.[27] SBA provided the loan approval and loan amount data to the Congressional Research Service (CRS), as they are not publically available. Qualitative data on SBA's trade-related programs are limited, but publically available survey responses are presented. This qualitative data include surveys commissioned by SBA and small business trade associations on the visibility, utilization, and outcomes of SBA's loan, management, and training programs.

Loan Programs

SBA has three loan programs that are specifically targeted toward exporters, and many of SBA's broader loan programs also support export-related activities. A brief description of SBA's non-export focused business loan programs is included in **Appendix**.

Table 3 displays the number of SBA-approved loans for export activities, for FY2011 to FY2013.[28] As shown in **Table 3**, SBA has approved approximately 1,500 loan guarantees annually over the three-year period. Export-supporting loans were a 2.5% ($924.9 million) share of all 7(a) and 504/CDC loan amounts in FY2011, 2.7% in FY2012 ($926.7 million), and 2.9% ($1.2 billion) in FY2013. These loan guarantees include loans that were serviced through SBA's three major export promotion-focused programs as well as SBA's non-export promotion-focused programs.

---

[25] Small Business Administration Office of Inspector General, *The SBA Need to Improve Its Management of the State Trade and Export Promotion Grant Program*, Report No. 12-21, September 25, 2012, at http://www.sba.gov/sites/default/files/Audit%20Report%2012-21%20Review%20of%20STEP%20Grant%20Program.pdf.

[26] Ibid.

[27] Small Business Administration, Office of Entrepreneurial Development, "Impact Study of Entrepreneurial Dynamics: Office of Entrepreneurial Development Resource Partners' Face-to-Face Counseling," September 2012, at http://www.sba.gov/sites/default/files/files/SBA_Converted_2012_d.pdf.

[28] "Loans approved" by SBA differ from "loans disbursed" by SBA, whereas the latter represents the actual amount of SBA support that goes towards small businesses. Some small-business owners that are approved for an SBA loan do not receive the funds for a variety of reasons: they find credit elsewhere, their business shuts down, etc. Thus, disbursements are always lower than approvals.

Table 3. SBA Approved Loans for Export-Related Activity, FY2011 to FY2013

Performance Measure	FY2011[a]	FY2012	FY2013
Number of Export-Related Loans	1,546	1,478	1,586
Number of Export-Related Loans as a Share of All 7(a) and 504/CDC Loans	2.5%	2.7%	2.9%
Amount of Export-Related Loans (in millions)	$924.9	$926.7	$1,190.5
Amount of Export-Related Loans as a Share of all 7(a) and 505/CDC Loans	3.8%	4.2%	5.2%

Source: U.S. Small Business Administration (SBA) data provided to the Congressional Research Service (CRS).

Notes: Loan amounts and values are reported for all approved loans, not all disbursed loans. Given that some borrowers cancel loans (for various reasons), the disbursed loan amounts are expected to be smaller than approved loan amounts.

Table 4 disaggregates the total number of loans approved for export-related activities by loan program. In general, no single loan program was responsible for the majority of SBA's export-related loans during the time covered by the data. The majority of loans were issued under programs outside of the three export-focused loan programs. When added together, the three export-focused loan programs comprised 32% of loans approved in FY2011, 28% in FY2012, and 32% in FY2013. Among SBA's various business loan programs, the highest share of export-focused loans were made under the SBA*Express* program. SBA's Preferred Lenders (a subset of the standard 7(a) loan program) was responsible for third-largest share of loan approvals in FY2011 (16%) and the second-largest share in FY2012 (18%) and FY2013 (16%).

Table 4. SBA Loan Program Approvals for Export-Related Activity, by Loan Program, FY2011-FY2013

Loan Program	FY2011[a] Loans Approved	FY2011[a] Share of Export Loans	FY2012 Loans Approved	FY2012 Share of Export Loans	FY2013 Loans Approved	FY2013 Share of Export Loans
SBAExpress	497	32%	413	28%	416	26%
Preferred Lenders Program (PLP)	250	16%	259	18%	251	16%
Export Express	287	19%	185	13%	160	10%
Export Working Capital	171	11%	159	11%	188	12%
Other 7(a)	134	9%	149	10%	141	9%
Accredited Lenders Program (ALP)	63	4%	95	6%	96	6%
International Trade	27	2%	61	4%	152	10%
504/CDC	38	2%	27	2%	41	3%
Patriot Express	36	2%	30	2%	23	1%
504/CDC Refinancing Option	2	<1%	37	3%	NA	NA
Gulf Opportunity (GO) Zone	3	<1%	27	2%	7	<1%
Small Loan Advantage (SLA)	NA	NA	17	1%	89	6%
Certified Lenders Program (CLP)	4	<1%	7	<1%	9	1%
Rural Lenders Program (RLA)	5	<1%	7	<1%	3	<1%
Community Advantage (CA)	NA	NA	5	<1%	10	1%
Community Express[b]	29	2%	NA	NA	NA	NA
Total	1,546	100%	1,478	100%	1,586	100%

Source: Analysis of SBA data provided to CRS.

a. Percentages may not add up to 100% in each fiscal year due to rounding.

b. The Community Express program stopped operations after FY2011 and was replaced with the SLA and CA loan programs beginning in FY2012.

Table 5 disaggregates the total amount of the loans approved for export-related activities by loan program. As with the number of loans approved, the majority of total, export-related loan amounts were issued under programs outside of the three export-focused loan programs. The SBA*Express* and Export Express programs account for a smaller share of total loan amounts than total loan numbers, primarily because the maximum cap on the amount of these loans is lower than most other SBA loan programs.

As shown in **Table 5**, the Export Working Capital program accounts for the highest share of the amount of credit approved annually by the SBA to small business exporters (29% in FY2011, 24% in FY2012, and 25% in FY2013). The three export-focused loan programs accounted for 36%, 40%, and 49% of export-related loan approval amounts in FY2011, FY2012, and FY2013, respectively. The Preferred Lenders Program also accounted for over 20% of the loan amounts approved annually over the same period.

Table 5. SBA Loan Program Approval Amounts for Export-Related Activity, by Loan Program, FY2011- FY2013

Loan Program	FY2011a Amount (millions)	FY2011a Share of Export Loans	FY2012 Amount (millions)	FY2012 Share of Export Loans	FY2013 (as of May 26, 2013) Amount (millions)	FY2013 (as of May 26, 2013) Share of Export Loans
Export Working Capital	$265.9	29%	$219.6	24%	$295.7	25%
Preferred Lenders Program (PLP)	$231.2	25%	$217.6	23%	$245.3	21%
Other 7(a)	$183.6	20%	$153.6	17%	$168.5	14%
International Trade	$31.2	3%	$97.0	10%	$251.1	21%
Accredited Lenders Program (ALP)	$40.1	4%	$84.4	9%	$80.2	7%
SBAExpress	$101.9	11%	$56.7	6%	$53.4	4%
Export Express	$36.2	4%	$35.2	4%	$30.9	3%
504	$23.4	3%	$18.3	2%	$30.8	3%
504 Refinancing Option	$2.4	<1%	$29.9	3%	NA	NA
Certified Lenders Program (CLP)	$2.2	<1%	$5.2	1%	$13.1	1%
Patriot Express	$4.4	<1%	$4.2	<1%	$3.2	<1%
Small Loan Advantage (SLA)	NA	NA	$1.7	<1%	$15.5	1%
Gulf Opportunity (GO) Zone	$0.2	<1%	$1.5	<1%	$0.4	<1%
Rural Lenders Program (RLA)	$1.4	<1%	$1.1	<1%	$0.7	<1%
Community Advantage (CA)	NA	NA	$0.7	<1%	$1.6	<1%
Community Expressb	$0.8	<1%	NA	NA	NA	NA
Total	**$924.9**	**100%**	**$926.7**	**100%**	**$1,190.5**	**100%**

Source: Analysis of SBA data provided to CRS.

a. Amounts and percentages for each category may not add up to totals in each fiscal year due to rounding.

b. The Community Express program stopped operations after FY2011 and was replaced with the SLA and CA loan programs beginning in FY2012.

In FY2012, the latest available data, SBA reported that OIT assisted 1,283 small business exporters to access capital through its export loan program. This is slightly less than the 1,346 small business exporters SBA assisted in FY2011 and the 1,326 exporters assisted in FY2010.[29] According to the U.S. Census Bureau, there were 177,948 firms with fewer than 500 employees that exported in calendar year 2011 and 174,652 firms in calendar year 2010.[30] Although the

---

[29] The SBA also reported that it assisted 3,167 small business exporters to access capital in FY2008 and 3,200 exporters in FY2007. See U.S. Small Business Administration, *FY2014 Congressional Budget Justification and FY2012 Annual Performance Report*, p. 62, at http://www.sba.gov/sites/default/files/files/1-508-Compliant-FY-2014-CBJ%20FY%202012%20APR.pdf.

[30] This does *not* include firms that were missing employment data, nonemployers (i.e., self-employed), and companies that reported annual payroll but did not report any employees on their payroll during specified period(s) in 2010 or 2011. See U.S. Census Bureau, *A Profile of U.S. Importing and Exporting Companies, 2010-2011*, April 5, 2013, p. 15, at http://www.census.gov/foreign-trade/Press-Release/edb/2011/edbrel.pdf.

measurement periods are not exactly the same (fiscal versus calendar year), it can be approximated that SBA's export portfolio comprised less than 1% of small business exporters in 2010 or 2011.

SBA does not publish data on the value of the exports supported by SBA loan programs.

Survey Responses

Since 2003, the SBA's Office of Entrepreneurial Development has commissioned an annual "multi-year time series study to assess the impact of the programs it offers to small businesses."[31] The survey asks questions about several aspects of the client's experiences with these programs, including the impact of the programs on their staffing decisions and management practices. The survey is sent each year to a stratified random sample of clients participating in the three largest SBA management and training programs: Small Business Development Centers (SBDCs), Women's Business Centers (WBCs), and SCORE (also known as the Service Corps of Retired Executives).[32] The survey responses are published by the SBA and include the responses of clients with a wide range of small business ownership and management experience.

The 2013 survey was sent to 29,957 SBDC clients, 2,997 WBC clients, and 25,183 SCORE clients in March 2013 to "provide an analysis of client attitudes toward their counseling experiences and client perceptions of the impact of that counseling on their businesses."[33] Of the 64,470 surveys sent, researchers received 9,459 responses (a 16% response rate).[34] The survey labels these three SBA programs as "resource partners." The latest survey findings were released in September 2013.

In general, the surveys indicate that these programs assisted small businesses at all stages of development, that most of the small business owners who participated in these programs and responded to the survey found them useful, most changed their management practices or strategies as a result of their participation.[35]

Relatively few survey respondents reported that they had sought information and counseling related to international trade. Among all of the survey participants, interactions with SBA resource partners most often led to a business plan (54% among survey respondents), a marketing plan (45%), or changes to general management (35%). In contrast, 4% of survey respondents

---

[31] U.S. Small Business Administration, Office of Entrepreneurial Development, "Impact Study of Entrepreneurial Development Resources," September 10, 2009, p. 2, at http://archive.sba.gov/idc/groups/public/documents/sba_program_office/ed_finalreport_2009.pdf.

[32] For more information on these programs, see CRS Report R41352, *Small Business Management and Technical Assistance Training Programs*, by Robert Jay Dilger.

[33] U.S. Small Business Administration, Office of Entrepreneurial Development, "Impact Study of Entrepreneurial Dynamics: Office of Entrepreneurial Development Resource Partners' Face-to-Face Counseling," September 2013, p. 10, at http://www.sba.gov/sites/default/files/files/OED_ImpactReport_09302013_Final.pdf.

[34] More specifically, there were 5,460 SBDC client respondents (18% response rate); 3,470 SCORE client respondents (14% response rate); and 340 WBC client respondents (18% response rate). Ibid., p. 8.

[35] Ibid., pp. 19-21. For more analysis of these surveys, see CRS Report R41352, *Small Business Management and Technical Assistance Training Programs*, by Robert Jay Dilger; and CRS Report R43083, *SBA Assistance to Small Business Startups: Client Experiences and Program Impact*, by Robert Jay Dilger.

reported that SBA resource partners delivered assistance concerning international trade (up from 2% in the 2012 survey).[36]

Given the few trade-specific questions in this SBA-commissioned survey, it is difficult to draw conclusions concerning the low shares of international trade-related outcomes among clients of the largest SBA management and training programs. One interpretation could be that few small businesses have the desire to export, thus few small businesses sought out counseling on how to increase exports. Others could claim that the focus of performance management analysis of international trade programs should be on small business *exporters* rather than SBA's small business clients more generally.

Surveys conducted in 2010 and 2013 jointly by the National Small Business Association (NSBA) and Small Business Exporters Association (SBEA), two trade groups, reported slightly higher interaction between exporters and the SBA than the SBA-commissioned study. Still, these surveys reinforce the notion that small business exporters are seeking out export-related advice from a variety of different sources.[37] **Table 6** compares the SBA-relevant information in these surveys.

---

[36] Among the 2012 survey participants, interactions with SBA resource partners most often led to a business plan (among 34% of survey respondents in 2011), a marketing plan (29%), or a financial strategy (20%). In contrast, only 2% of survey respondents reported that SBA resource partners delivered assistance concerning international trade. No 2012 survey respondents who were clients of WBCs reported that SBA resource partners delivered assistance concerning international trade. See U.S. Small Business Administration, *Impact Study of Entrepreneurial Dynamics: Office of Entrepreneurial Development Resource Partners' Face-to-Face Counseling*, September 2012, pp. 27 and 65, at http://www.sba.gov/sites/default/files/files/SBA_Converted_2012_d.pdf.

[37] National Small Business Association and Small Business Exporters Association, *2010 Small Business Exporting Survey*, 2010, pp. 7 and 4, at http://www.nsba.biz/docs/2010_small_business_exporting_survey_001.pdf; and 2013 Small Business Exporting Survey, 2013, at http://www nsba.biz/wp-content/uploads/2013/06/Exporting-Survey-2013.pdf. For survey methodologies, see the specific reports. The 2010 survey is representative of 250 exporting and non-exporting members of NSBA and SBEA. The 2013 survey is representative of 500 exporting and non-exporting members of NSBA and SBEA.

Table 6. Exporter Survey Responses on SBA International Trade Programs

	2010a	2013
SBA-Managed Programs		
Am aware of Small Business Development Centers (generally)b	64%	58%
Received exporting advice from a Small Business Development Center	12%	13%
Received exporting advice from an SBA District Office	NA	8%
Am aware of SBA export lending programs	29%	43%
Taken advantage of SBA export lending programs	12%	3%
Program Partnerships Between SBA and Department of Commerce		
Am aware of U.S. Export Assistance Centers	18%	15%
Taken advantage of a U.S. Export Assistance Center in a major U.S. city	26%	10%

Source: National Small Business Association and Small Business Exporters Association, *2010 Small Business Exporting Survey*, 2010, pp. 4 and 7, at http://www.nsba.biz/docs/2010_small_business_exporting_survey_001.pdf; and *2013 Small Business Exporting Survey*, 2013, pp. 5 and 16, at http://www.nsba.biz/wp-content/uploads/2013/06/Exporting-Survey-2013.pdf.

a. For survey methodologies, see the specific reports. The 2010 survey included responses from 250 exporting and non-exporting members of NSBA and SBEA. The 2013 survey included responses from 500 exporting and non-exporting members of NSBA and SBEA. Only the responses for the exporting small businesses are summarized in this table.

b. The 2010 survey distinguished between "exporting assistance" provided by SBDCs and generally SBDC services. The responses in **Table 6** reflect affirmative responses to the latter. When asked if they had heard of SBDC exporting assistance services, 8% of survey respondents in 2010 responded affirmatively. The 2013 survey did not contain answers to this specific question.

According to the NSBA/SBEA surveys, 64% of small business exporters were aware of SBDCs in 2010 and 12% of them received exporting advice from SBDCs. In the 2013 survey, 58% of respondents were aware of SBDCs, and 13% had actually sought out exporting advice from SBDCs and 8% received exporting advice from an SBA district office. Although awareness of SBA export lending programs increased from 29% of respondents in 2010 to 43% in 2013, the share of respondents who actually took advantage of these programs decreased from 12% in 2010 to 3% in 2013 (perhaps due to the end of the STEP program).

Evaluations from the NSBA/SBEA surveys are mixed when comparing SBA programs with other federal programs. On the one hand, SBDCs were the ninth most used government program by small business exporters surveyed in 2010, and the second most used program in 2013 (even though the percentage of respondents who used SBDCs for exporting advice only changed from 12% to 13%).[38] On the other hand, presentations and websites from the U.S. Department of Commerce were used more often by survey respondents in both years than any of the SBA's programs.

---

[38] Many non-SBA programs exhibited a significant drop in utilization rates between the 2010 and 2013 NSBA/SBEA surveys, although it is not apparent why this happened.

Issues for Congress

This section of the report introduces three policy issues for consideration as Congress looks to the future size and scope of SBA's export promotion activities: (1) are there barriers to exporting or market failures impeding smaller firms from international trade? (2) is there a compelling interest for the government to promote exports in the name of national trade competitiveness? and (3) are SBA's export-promotion policies duplicative of other federal programs? These issues will likely be framed by the rising concerns about fiscal responsibility and sustained economic recovery.

Small Business Barriers to Exporting and Possible Market Failures

Proponents of federal support for small business exports argue that small businesses face inherent barriers to participating in international trade. Some of the commonly cited barriers in academic literature include

- not enough capacity to export,
- not enough information or lack of awareness of services available,
- logistical difficulties in international distribution,
- difficulties in export marketing,
- difficulties in obtaining export financing,
- no perceived demand abroad,
- bureaucratic processes and regulations (i.e., "red-tape"), and
- no desire to export.[39]

Restricted access to credit is also indicative of a barrier to small business exports. A survey of the empirical literature suggests that access to finance and the cost of credit do not only pose barriers to small business trade financing in many countries (including the United States), but also constrain small businesses more than large firms.[40] Smaller firms often find it difficult to obtain commercial bank financing (especially long-term loans) for a number of reasons, including lack of collateral, difficulties in proving creditworthiness, inadequate credit history, small cash flows, higher risk premiums, underdeveloped bank-borrower relationships, and high transaction costs.

---

[39] For a discussion of studies that examine each of these commonly-cited barriers to small business exports, see Kurt J. Miesenbock, "Small Business and Exporting: A Literature Review," *International Small Business Journal*, vol. 6, no. 2 (1988), pp. 42-61; and U.S. International Trade Commission, *Small and Medium-Sized Enterprises: Overview of Participation in U.S. Exports*, Investigation No. 332-508, January 2010, pp. 2-15 to 2-16, at http://www.usitc.gov/publications/332/pub4125.pdf.

[40] See Joe Peek, *The Impact of Credit Availability on Small Business Exporters*, Small Business Administration Office of Advocacy, April 2013, at http://www.sba.gov/sites/default/files/files/rs404tot%283%29.pdf. For cross-national studies see International Finance Corporation (IFC), *The SME Banking Knowledge Guide*, 2010, http://www1.ifc.org/wps/wcm/connect/industry_ext_content/ifc_external_corporate_site/industries/financial+markets/publications/toolkits/smebknowledge+guide; Bert Scholtens, "Analytical Issues in External Financing Alternatives for SMEs," *Small Business Economics*, vol. 12 (1999), pp. 137-148; and Thorsten Beck et al., "The Determinants of Financing Obstacles," *Journal of International Money and Finance*, vol. 25, no. 6 (2006), pp. 932-952. However, consistency among national indicators limits extensive comparisons of SME financing across countries.

These problems are typically compounded, even relative to larger firms, by events such as the recent financial crisis.

In general, economic theory suggests export promotion programs increase economic inefficiencies and reduce national welfare. Specifically, economic theory indicates that in most instances firms and workers will locate to the most efficient and productive areas to do business in the long run, without the assistance of government policy. From this perspective, government policies, such as export promotion programs, that create incentives to engage in one form of economic activity, potentially at the expense of another, results in net social loss of economic efficiency—where finite resources are not being used to produce their maximum output for the lowest cost.[41] Economic theory indicates that these policies create a distortion in the market, such that resources are directed from an area of higher productivity to an area of lower productivity.

On the other hand, most economists believe that some government assistance could be justified in the presence of a *market failure*, where the market is unable to efficiently allocate resources on its own. If there is indeed a presence of a market failure, then there could be an economic basis for small business export promotion programs (assuming the costs of these programs were less than aggregate increase in economic activity).

Although studies indicate that smaller firms face barriers to exporting, many of these conditions are not necessarily indicative of a market failure. Higher risk profiles for small exporters could be justified by their higher rates of failure, and compounded by their ability to absorb risks associated with international transactions (e.g., currency fluctuations, transportation costs). Incomplete information among small businesses concerning the benefits of internationalization and how to internationalize their business could be indicative of a market failure, though, particularly if more information could allow small businesses to operate more efficiently and increase competition.

Small Business Exports and U.S. Trade "Competitiveness"

There has been an ongoing debate among economists and business experts about the theoretical basis linking trade competitiveness to economic outcomes. Most economic policy experts agree that the major determinant of economic growth is domestic productivity growth (e.g., net increases in investment, labor supply, or technology that allows for a more efficient use of capital or labor). However, there is a divide among other experts concerning the merits of encouraging the development of sectors that produce tradable goods and services as a means to improve net exports, increase jobs, and encourage productivity growth.

Proponents of national trade competitiveness theory believe that individual countries have a compelling policy interest to increase the real (inflation-adjusted) income of their citizens, often times through promoting growth in specific, tradable sectors.[42] Supporters of trade

---

[41] Economists typically view the most efficient means of production as the one that provides the most benefit at the lowest cost.

[42] Some point to persistent trade deficits and the corresponding increase in U.S. international indebtedness as an indication of a decline in the long-run competitiveness of the United States. However, these conditions do not necessarily lead to a decline in standards of living (e.g., real GDP). See Lawrence R. Klein, "Components of Competitiveness," *Science*, vol. 241, no. 4863 (July 15, 1988), pp. 308-318; and George N. Hatospoulos, Paul R. Krugman, and Lawrence H. Summers, "U.S. Competitiveness: Beyond the Trade Deficit," *Science*, vol. 241, no. 4863 (July 15, 1988), pp. 299-307.

competitiveness theory are largely focused on strategies that guide individual businesses in the marketplace.[43] These firm-level strategies are then applied to the national level to inform public policy. Specifically, government policy can either reduce a business's profit (e.g., through national regulations) or increase a business's bottom-line (e.g., by subsidizing production) such that domestic firms in the near-term can have a higher financial profit in a head-to-head "competition" with their international competitors. Loss of competitiveness, these advocates claim, will lead to the loss of American jobs, the movement of U.S. business operations overseas, reduced investment by foreign businesses in the United States, etc.

Some view a strong network of small businesses as being critical for U.S. economic competitiveness in the international market. In part, this notion comes from the belief that small businesses are the primary source of job creation in the United States, and access to international markets could further increase the number of jobs created by small businesses. In a related argument, proponents of small business exports say that small businesses are critical for innovative, international supply chains. For example, in an article for the *Washington Post*, former-SBA Administrator Karen Mills described small businesses supply chain networks with larger firms and small businesses' innovations in production as being important in the promotion of U.S. international economic competitiveness.[44]

In contrast, economic theory generally does not support international competitiveness as a national policy goal. A 1994 article by economist Paul Krugman provides an argument against trade competitiveness theory based on the economic theory of competitive advantage.[45] In summary, Krugman argues that firms might *compete* with one another, but countries *trade* with each other. To support this statement, Krugman says that firms go out of business when they fail to compete in the marketplace, but countries do not. When a country fails to be "competitive" in a particular industry, national resources (e.g., capital, labor) are then used toward production in a different industry. Krugman argues that this process allows for a more efficient allocation of resources, because countries are guided by market signals to specialize in the industry where they possess a "comparative advantage" instead of using government resources to provide incentives for economic activity in an industry where they are relatively less efficient in production. In summary, Krugman reaffirms traditional economic theories that say that government policies that promote employment in certain sectors redirects employment from other sectors, and that productivity gain (in the form of higher wages) for workers in the "higher-valued" industries is passed along to other workers in the form of higher prices (and lower productivity).[46]

Even if other countries are providing government incentives for their national small businesses to export, then some economists would still say that Krugman's thesis holds. According to this logic, the United States should not engage in policies that lead to an inefficient allocation of resources and net loss in national welfare because its trading partners do so. Others expand upon Krugman's theoretical reasoning by arguing that the drive for national "competitiveness," relative to another country, could be used to justify trade protectionism, restrict capital or labor mobility, increase

---

[43] For a sample of scholars on U.S. competitiveness theory, see Harvard Business School, *U.S. Competitiveness Project*, at http://www.hbs.edu/competitiveness/overview.html.

[44] Karen Mills, "U.S. competitiveness hinges on the strength of small business suppliers," *The Washington Post*, May 6, 2013, at http://www.washingtonpost.com/business/on-small-business/sbas-karen-mills-us-competitiveness-hinges-on-the-strength-of-small-business-suppliers/2013/05/06/03f517b8-b412-11e2-9a98-4be1688d7d84_story.html.

[45] See Paul R. Krugman, "Competitiveness: A Dangerous Obsession," *Foreign Affairs*, vol. 73, no. 2 (March/April 1994).

[46] Paul R. Krugman, "Proving My Point," *Foreign Affairs*, vol. 73, no. 4 (July/August 1994).

unemployment by sending political signals of support for certain industries, or engage in "beggar-thy-neighbor" policies of international retaliation that consume national resources.[47]

Duplication of Services

In the past, Congress has passed legislation to increase export promotion programs targeted toward small business across various federal agencies. For example, Congress has increased minimum percentage targets of the Export-Import Bank's (Ex-Im's) aggregate loan, guarantee, and insurance authority for financing exports by small businesses over the past 30 years.[48] The Export-Import Bank Reauthorization Act of 2006 (P.L. 109-438) required the President of Ex-Im to establish and maintain a Small Business Division. As previously mentioned, Congress elevated the goal of export promotion, within SBA, when it established an Assistant Administrator to head the Office of International Trade in the Small Business Jobs Act of 2010 (P.L. 111-240).

More recently, though, the possible overlap and duplication of services across federal agencies that support export promotion programs for small business has become a concern for some Members of Congress. These concerns are largely driven by desires for more efficient delivery of government services, reductions in spending, and elimination of duplicative programs.

The Government Accountability Office (GAO) identified overlap of services between SBA's export promotion activities and other federal agencies. GAO has compared SBA's programs with those at Ex-Im and various parts of the Department of Commerce.[49] Particularly, GAO noted that SBDCs and Commerce provide some similar one-on-one counseling services to small businesses, and SBA and Ex-Im offer overlapping loan guarantee programs through similar lending institutions. SBA and Commerce responded to these claims by saying that each agency tends to target different audiences by specializing in areas where they have more experience. For example, Commerce works more with existing small business exporters to expand their range of products and services to more markets, whereas SBA works more with small businesses that are looking to begin to export.

After conducting interviews with government officials and private-sector representatives, a 2013 GAO report concluded that overlap in services led to confusion for some small businesses. SBA and Commerce noted that both agencies have begun to clarify counseling roles and responsibilities through an interagency communiqué.[50] GAO recommended that SBA consult with Ex-Im and Commerce more closely to provide specific guidance among the agencies' export promotion counseling to small business, and to identify ways to share client information. SBA

---

[47] Rudolf Scharping, "Rule-Based Competition," *Foreign Affairs*, vol. 73, no. 4 (July/August 1994).

[48] The Supplemental Appropriations Act, 1984 (P.L. 98-181) required Ex-Im to make available for FY1986 and thereafter not less than 10% of its aggregate loan, guarantee, and insurance authority for financing exports by small businesses. The Export-Import Bank Reauthorization Act of 2002 (P.L. 107-189) increased this minimum annual percentage to 20% in subsequent fiscal years. Ex-Im uses SBA's size standards methodology to determine whether a company qualifies as a small business.

[49] See Appendix I in U.S. Government Accountability Office, *2013 Annual Report: Actions Needed to Reduce Fragmentation, Overlap, Duplication, and Achieve Other Financial Benefits*, GAO-13-279SP, April 2013, p. 232, at http://www.gao.gov/assets/660/653604.pdf; and U.S. Government Accountability Office, *Small Business Administration Needs to Implement Its Expanded Role*, GAO-13-217, January 2013, at http://www.gao.gov/assets/660/651685.pdf.

[50] U.S. Government Accountability Office, *Small Business Administration Needs to Implement Its Expanded Role*, GAO-13-217, January 2013, at http://www.gao.gov/assets/660/651685.pdf.

has been responsive to some of GAO's concerns, but it has noted that legislation generally prevents SBA from sharing specific client information outside of the agency without prior consent.[51] GAO also recommended that SBA and Ex-Im may be able to explore options to harmonize export financing products and to assist lenders in more easily adapting to the rules for both agencies' products. In any case, co-location of some of these services (in the form of U.S. Export Assistance Centers) could help to reduce the burdens on small businesses in obtaining comprehensive, export counseling assistance.

Improving export program efficiencies have been the focus of several recent bills and could also become a larger issue if Congress grants the President the authority to reorganize certain business- and trade-related offices (and entire agencies) across the federal government under a single agency. Most recently, the President has reiterated his call for this authority in his FY2014 budget recommendation.[52] SBA has been named as one agency whose trade-related functions could be consolidated under the President's proposal.

In the 112th Congress, the Reforming and Consolidating Government Act of 2012 (S. 2129) would have provided the President with much of this authority.

In the 113th Congress, several bills have been introduced to help small businesses exporters, including the following:

- The Export Coordination Act of 2013 (H.R. 1909) would help to clarify the role of each federal agency in each part of the export process.

- The TRADE (Transparent Rules Allow Direct Exporting) for Small Businesses and Jobs Act (H.R. 1916) would help small businesses increase their exports and enter new markets by helping companies better understand foreign regulations and directing trade agencies to monitor and collect up-to-date information on changes to tariff and non-tariff laws, regulations, and practices, and display them in a clear and easy to read format.[53]

- The Small Business Export Growth Act (S. 1179) would encourage greater coordination between state and federal resources by creating a working group on the Trade Promotion Coordinating Committee (TPCC) to streamline efforts among state and federal export promotion and assistance agencies, identify opportunities to consolidate unnecessary government offices, and require SBA to conduct greater export outreach to small businesses.

- The State Trade Coordination Act of 2013 (H.R. 1926) would require increase representation and integration of state trade programs into federal trade

---

[51] Ibid., p. 33.

[52] Office of Management and Budget, *Fiscal Year 2014 Budget of the U.S. Government*, April 2013, p. 50, at http://www.whitehouse.gov/sites/default/files/omb/budget/fy2014/assets/budget.pdf. For more analysis on executive branch reorganization initiatives, see CRS Report R41841, *Executive Branch Reorganization Initiatives During the 112th Congress: A Brief Overview*, by Henry B. Hogue; CRS Report R42555, *Trade Reorganization: Overview and Issues for Congress*, by Shayerah Ilias Akhtar; and CRS Report R42852, *Presidential Reorganization Authority: History, Recent Initiatives, and Options for Congress*, by Henry B. Hogue.

[53] For a more detailed summary of each piece of legislation, see House Small Business Committee Chairman Sam Graves (MO), "Committee Members Introduce No-Cost Legislation To Help Small Business Enter Trade Market," press release, May 9, 2013, at http://smallbusiness.house.gov/news/documentsingle.aspx?DocumentID=333026.

promotion programs, and establish information sharing and reporting metrics between the states and the federal government.

As of the publication date of this report, only the State Trade Coordination Act of 2013 (H.R. 1926) has been reported out of committee. On June 26, 2013, the House Foreign Affairs Committee's Subcommittee on Terrorism, Nonproliferation and Trade ordered (by voice vote) H.R. 1926 to be reported to the House floor.[54]

---

[54] For media coverage of the voice, see Elham Khatami, "Export Promotion Bills Backed by Panel," *CQ Roll Call*, June 26, 2013, at http://www.cq.com/doc/committees-20130626003094422?wr=eFF6UlQqRXM3azJVd1NSLTdJR1Fjdw.

Appendix. A Brief Description of SBA Loan Programs Used to Support Export Activities

- **7(a) Loan Program:** SBA's flagship loan guaranty program for working capital.
  - *SBAExpress:* Expedited review process for 7(a) with more restrictive loan limits.
  - *Patriot Express:* Expedited review process with higher maximum loan amounts and lower maximum interest rates than SBAExpress. Eligible only to veterans, active-duty military members, reservists, and their spouses.
  - *Export Express:* Similar to SBAExpress. Eligible to businesses that intend to internationalize or expand their current export operations.
  - *Export Working Capital Program:* Short-term working capital loans for exporters.
  - *International Trade Export Program:* Term loan for permanent working capital related to international trade.
  - *Community Advantage (CA):* Targets community-based and mission-based financial institutions.
  - *Community Express:* Expedited review process for CA program with more restrictive loan limits.
  - *Small Loan Advantage (SLA):* Expedited review process for smaller loans in underserved communities.
  - *Preferred Lenders Program (PLP):* SBA delegates the final credit decision and most servicing and liquidation authority and responsibility to carefully selected PLP lenders.
  - *Rural Lenders Program (RLA):* Streamlined review process for smaller loans made by rural lenders.
- **504/CDC Loan Program:** Provides loan guarantees to Certified Development Companies (CDCs) for long-term fixed-asset loans (i.e., non-working capital). Has job creation requirements.
  - *Accredited Lenders Program (ALP):* SBA gives certain lenders increased authority to process, close, and service 504/CDC loans, and provides expedited processing of loan approval and servicing actions.
  - *Certified Lenders Program (CLP):* SBA designates qualified CDCs as Premier CLP CDCs and delegates to them increased authority to process, close, service, and liquidate 504/CDC loans.
  - *504/CDC Refinancing Option:* Allowed refinancing of existing 504/CDC loans for purposes beyond business expansion (program ended in Sept. 2012)
- **Gulf Opportunity (GO) Zone:** Provides disaster loans for small business owners affected by Hurricane Katrina.

For more information, see CRS Report RL33243, *Small Business Administration: A Primer on Programs*, by Robert Jay Dilger and Sean Lowry; and Small Business Administration, *Loan Program Quick Reference Guide*, June 2012, at http://www.sba.gov/content/loan-program-quick-reference-guide.

Author Contact Information

Sean Lowry
Analyst in Public Finance
slowry@crs.loc.gov, 7-9154

www.ingramcontent.com/pod-product-compliance
Lightning Source LLC
Chambersburg PA
CBHW081822170526

45167CB00008B/3507